READ
to me
TALK
to me
LISTEN
to me

READ
to me
TALK
to me
LISTEN
to me

Your Child's
First Three Years

NANCY DEVLIN, PH.D.

authorHOUSE®

AuthorHouse™
1663 Liberty Drive
Bloomington, IN 47403
www.authorhouse.com
Phone: 1 (800) 839-8640

Published by AuthorHouse 08/04/2015

ISBN: 978-1-5049-2333-0 (sc)
ISBN: 978-1-5049-2332-3 (e)

Print information available on the last page.

Any people depicted in stock imagery provided by Thinkstock are models,
and such images are being used for illustrative purposes only.
Certain stock imagery © Thinkstock.

This book is printed on acid-free paper.

Because of the dynamic nature of the Internet, any web addresses or links contained in
this book may have changed since publication and may no longer be valid. The views
expressed in this work are solely those of the author and do not necessarily reflect the
views of the publisher, and the publisher hereby disclaims any responsibility for them.

CONTENTS

1

Introduction

We know the country has a problem when a woman says: "I don't work." "I'm just a stay-at-home mother." Or even, "I'm just a housewife." These words are said humbly and apologetically in answer to the question, "What do you do?"

"Just a mother" is the highest calling one can have. The problem is that no one believes this: not the mother, not the workplace and not the government.

We know the mother does not believe it because even before the baby is born, plans have been made for somebody else to take care of him. This, in spite of the fact that all of the studies unequivocally find that what is best for the baby is for his mother to nurture and if possible to breast feed him for at least the first six months.

We know that the workplace does not believe this because a law had to be passed before employers would give mothers the right to stay home in order to nurture their new babies. The "Family and Medical Leave Act" allows mothers to take up to twelve unpaid weeks off, without risking their jobs, to care for the newborn baby. Many employers do not inform their employees of their rights under this law nor do they post the notice as required by law.

Even when informed, many women do not take advantage of the law because they fear it will affect their careers and future earnings if they take off six months, let alone three years to raise their child. This, in spite of the fact that women live longer and will be in the work force longer. Three years seems a short time to take out of a career that can span over thirty or forty years.

We know that the government does not believe this because it is willing to subsidize day care but not mother care. In the case of the welfare mother, it is making it impossible for her to stay home with her new baby. The government, in compiling its statistics, does not acknowledge the productive work of the mother and her contribution to the economy since what she contributes is unremunerated. Only paid work is recognized and recorded. In case the men who originate these rules and develop these statistics have not noticed, motherhood IS work.

Day care, no matter how well done, is no substitute for the parent. The mother is critical for the first six months and essential for the first three years.

A mother knows her baby best. The baby thrives with the mother who smothers him with love and who is always there for him. A baby needs one-to-one attention and has difficulty relating to the many, often unfamiliar, adults he encounters in day care. In order to thrive, babies need permanence, continuity, passion and commitment. A mother has these qualities in abundance. Let us all strive to help her to do her job and to be what the world needs most --"just a mother."

2

Politicians

Many candidates for president do not seem to have a good education agenda. This could be because they know too little about the topic to have any agenda. The following is an attempt to educate them for the future.

Of all creatures, humans at birth are the least equipped with innate mechanisms needed for survival. Their brains are not fully developed. This makes them amazingly adaptable but exceedingly vulnerable requiring a huge investment by the adults who care for them.

It also forces each baby to go through the process of development, which can only be done by acting on and reacting to the environment. Babies, when stimulated, rapidly learn to influence their environment, to adapt it to themselves and to learn about it by exploring it. Every baby needs to experience this in order for the brain to develop and for learning to take place.

The basic building blocks for the baby's future development are laid from birth to age three because of the plasticity of the brain at these ages. If the brain is not stimulated during that time, as one researcher put it, the "windows of opportunity" are permanently closed. Age three or five, when children go to school, is too late. Children who have not been stimulated are already at a disadvantage and may never catch up.

Babies who began life ready to explore and to live the great adventure are easily defeated by adults who discourage their inquisitiveness and who do not express joy in each new achievement. These babies eventually give up and become lackadaisical. Some babies are left in playpens with bottles in their mouths and the television on for long periods of time by caretakers who are overwhelmed.

Politicians, instead of making educational policies about getting tough with students and the educational establishment, (which is like closing the barn door after the horses have escaped) should be making policies about prevention. The damage has been done before the child comes to school.

Get-tough pronouncements that demand that welfare mothers go to work forces them to depend on day care. These women are taken out of their homes and away from their children with little to show for it because of the high cost of this day care. Instead of these get-tough policies, politicians would be doing the babies a favor by setting up a program to educate the mothers so that they have the opportunity to provide the stimulating environment the babies so desperately need.

Instead of punishing welfare mothers by forcing them out of the home, a system should be developed whereby welfare mothers could stay home and still get their benefits. All politicians need to understand child development if they are going to make decisions that affect the welfare of the family. They need to understand that many children are not succeeding in school because their "windows of opportunity" for intellectual, physical, social and emotional growth were closed long before they arrived at the school door.

Politicians of good faith, please remember the children. They are our only hope for the future.

3

Motherhood as a Profession

Being an at-home mother especially during a baby's first three years of life has to be raised to the status of a profession like doctor, lawyer and teacher. As in any profession, in order to be licensed to practice, one has to finish a course of study and to complete an internship. After successfully completing training and entering the child-rearing profession, a mother, like every other professional, would receive a salary commensurate with her training and experience.

Sound far fetched? Maybe not. Maybe something as dramatic as giving motherhood the best the country has to give in terms of money, education, support and prestige is the only thing that is going to save our neglected children and ensure a brighter future for our country. In our status-conscious society, motherhood is about as low as you can get. At the top are athletes, movie stars, and other celebrities, who contribute little if anything to the country's well-being.

The reason motherhood should be given the high status of a profession is that every profession polices its members because all suffer when one performs badly. We suffer too. Deficient doctors endanger our lives. Deficient lawyers exaggerate our quarrels. Deficient teachers perpetuate our ignorance. And, as was pointed out by James Q. Wilson of UCLA, deficient parents produce poor citizens.

We cannot afford to continue to neglect our nation's babies. It is no longer a question of maybe or maybe not or when we get around to it. It is a question of our survival, not in the future, but NOW.

Mothers and teachers are in lonely professions. They are expected to spend most of their day with children, usually with little or no relief. Guiding children to become responsible adults is a noble calling and used to be very satisfying because mothers and teachers were respected for a job well-done. Our culture, however, no longer holds women who take on these roles in such esteem and their task has become difficult and isolated. Many women who would be excellent mothers and teachers are choosing other professions.

Society expects today's mothers to do the job alone. There is no support system for them. Mothers used to have grandparents and other relatives nearby whom they could count on to help. Grandmother lived within walking distance and the children could go on their own to visit her. Now grandparents may live half a continent away and probably have full time jobs. Often mothers lack even a friendly neighbor to visit for adult companionship or to share stories about each others children. The neighbors all go to work.

A mother once apologized to me because she was not working. (It is interesting that she did not equate staying at home to raise her children as work.) She felt inadequate and out of place in our modern society. I asked her how many children had her name down as the person the school should call in an emergency. She quickly added up in her head the names of sixteen children. Obviously she would have upset the equilibrium of the whole neighborhood if she had gone to work. A number of "working" mothers were counting on her. Unfortunately, so few women stay at home that the ones who do have no one to share the burden and this adds to the difficulty of their situation.

Parents of nursery school age children face a similar dilemma. Whether they want to or not they send their children to nursery school at a young age because there are no children left in the neighborhood for them to play with.

Teachers have some of the same needs as mothers who spend a great part of their day with children. Their work can be draining and exhausting. They need intellectual stimulation and meaningful contact with other adults, and like mothers, approval for what they are doing. They also should be provided with the opportunity of sharing their ideas and feelings with other adults. Teachers and today's "non-working" mothers are regarded as low in the "pecking order" in today's culture.

The recent focus on education and teachers may result in some relief for the teachers. There has not been similar focus on the problems of the lonely mothers. Until there is, more and more women will be persuaded to turn their energies and skills outward, away from their children, or to avoid motherhood entirely. I fear this bodes ill for the future of our children and our country.

4

Career and Children

It is time that we as a nation stop squandering our most precious resource--our children.

It is not enough for parents to bring children into the world and only provide food, clothing and shelter for them. Children also need to be nurtured, socialized and educated. If parents, for whatever reason, cannot fulfill this responsibility, then somebody else has to take over. Otherwise, the next generation will suffer.

The first thing that can be done is to make it easy, acceptable and pleasant for mothers to stay home with their children if they so desire especially for the first three years of the child's life. Career versus children does not have to be an either-or proposition. Women should not be put at a professional disadvantage in their careers in order to raise their children. The two are not incompatible. As a matter of fact, it is important that successful career women be given the opportunity to raise their children because they probably have much to offer them. One of the skills the baby acquires during this time is the ability to communicate and to use language. This skill is developed by close interaction with the adults in the environment. Language does not seem to be taught, but rather, it is caught by the baby being stimulated to communicate. Unless such stimulation occurs, receptive and expressive language acquisition may be impaired.

Parents who work are forced to depend on others to provide the necessary stimulation, encouragement, and nurturing needed for the baby's proper development. If this substitute care is not adequate, the baby's development may suffer. When this happens to enough babies, the nation suffers.

Probably one of the least paid are the people hired to take charge of young babies. It is almost impossible for the parents to supervise what is happening to their babies because they are at work. If this is their only or first child, they lack guidelines to know if their child is developing satisfactorily, or if they should be concerned because something is not right with the child. Sometimes the parents do not have enough experience to know what their child needs in the way of care in order for normal development to take place so they cannot judge the quality of the care the child is receiving.

One mother of an infant expressed concern when she realized that her baby was in a room with several other babies with the gate closed and the television turned on. They were not stimulated but were encouraged to sleep. Children in such environments are likely to fall behind others in more stimulating situations who have the warm, lively companionship of caring adults overseeing the children's exploration of their universe.

It is time the nation begins to realize that it needs to be concerned about supervision of childcare personnel. It is time to force employers to give time off to parents who want to raise their children without jeopardizing their job security. It is especially time for the nation to raise the role of parenting to the high level it deserves.

5

Development

Believe in yourself. You are the expert as far as your child is concerned. You know your child better than anyone and, based on this knowledge, you are well equipped to decide what is best for him. In order to do this, however, you need information about child development.

Babies come from the womb not fully developed. They make the greatest spurts in development in the first three years of their lives. During these spurts, they go full-speed-ahead unless someone or something stops them. And we let them, and rejoice in their every accomplishment.

There is no need to accelerate or delay an infant's rate of development. We cannot make a baby walk until he is ready to do so anyhow. A baby learns by actively exploring his environment. Keeping him in a crib or playpen in front of television prevents him from doing this. Babies whose urge to explore is thwarted fail to thrive, become passive, and never really develop a zest for learning. They rarely make up for the time lost in those first three years. I mention this in case your baby is in day care. Many day care services are well aware of these facts, and they are careful to encourage an infant's exploration. It is important for you to know if your child's day care center allows and encourages his explorations. We allow very young children to play and to develop in their own unique way usually until age three. Then we tend to intervene because "play time is over."

Some people are impatient for their child to learn at a very early age. After their child reaches three years, "learning", for many parents, means the things taught in school. They characterize anything else as play and regard it as waste of valuable time. Recent studies have shown that play is an important part of a child's development. In studies of animals, it was found that play stimulates circuits in the brain and helps to tame hostile impulses. The researchers believe the same is true for children. Play is so important to the growing child that parents should initiate it with their babies and encourage it thereafter. As the saying goes: "Play is the work of childhood."

Research also indicates that children who play alone or with others often become more creative and imaginative. Those who can be preoccupied for a long time with toys seem to be able to concentrate for longer periods of time as adults. Also, children who play regularly with peers seem to be better-adjusted adults and have developed good socialization skills.

Take very seriously a related saying: "All work and no play makes Jack a dull boy." School-type activities are usually imposed by adults, while play is usually created by the child, providing opportunity for self-discovery, creativity and use of the imagination. Some parents on hearing this might decide to introduce "mandatory play" as a way to foster their child's development. When adults attempt to control and to direct play, it is no longer play, and is rarely fun or helpful to the developing child.

We might try to bring back the spirit of play to all our endeavors. I encourage you to do it not only for your children, but for yourself. It would certainly make all of our lives more pleasant and less stressful.

6

First Three Years

Unlike most of the animals of the wild, born physically capable of taking care of their needs, the human child emerges from the womb unfinished. Much of his development takes place after birth in the extraordinary first three years of life. How the body and brain grows and develops during this period will affect the human child forever.

Our society is presently engaged in a furious controversy about protecting the child in the womb, but it is criminally negligent concerning the vital years following birth. What is so extraordinary about this knowledge is that its implications for future generations is ignored. Some of today's parents have children without intending to personally follow through with their children's development during this crucial time. They leave that to others.

That leaves the educational system with children who probably will never reach their full potential. By school age, scientists tell us, the plasticity of the brain is gone. We keep trying to make up for those years by many different kinds of school reforms. We bewail the fact that students do not seem to be as well prepared as they once were. We blame it on the curriculum and lack of behavioral and intellectual discipline, and we try to make appropriate adjustments. Nothing seems to change. Parents blame schools and teachers and demand that they do something for the students. What a pity. Nobody seems willing to protect and to nurture the very young child so that he has a brighter future.

Ultimately parents are responsible. Recent studies carried out over many years in six regions of North America found a consistent correlation between quality of family life and level of cognitive development during the first three years of life. Parental attentiveness and availability of stimulating play proved more strongly related to child development status than global measures of environmental quality such as socioeconomic status.

Enough is known about early child development to help parents become effective teachers of their developing children. One program, "Parents as First Teachers", was developed for the Missouri school system by Dr. Burton White, of the Center for Parent Education in Massachusetts. Parents enrolled in this program were helped from the third trimester of their pregnancy to their child's third birthday. The evaluation of this program indicated that these children scored significantly higher on all measures of intelligence, achievement, auditory comprehension, verbal ability and language ability than did comparison children. They also demonstrated more positive social development, including ability to work well with adults. These parents also were more likely than a comparison group to rate their school districts as responsive to their children's needs.

Several recommendations should be obvious from these data. Effective parenting skills can be learned. The best time to learn them is before becoming a parent. A course like "Parents as First Teachers" should be required of every high school student, both male and female. It could be one of the most important courses given in our schools. It should be a highly regarded course and it should be staffed with outstanding teachers.

The other recommendation is that businesses encourage their women employees, who choose to have children, to stay home with them for the first three years. These women should be assured that their job will be waiting for them when they return. It would be even better, if these mothers were subsidized so that staying home would not be a financial burden to the family. It seems strange that big businesses oppose this idea while at the same time they deplore the intellectual and educational deficiencies of their workers. They are forced to spend a great deal of money on remedial education. Why not spend some of that money on prevention? We are becoming a nation of people who do not care what happens to the next generation.

7

Play

Parents of preschool children are concerned about learning and want to provide the best for their children so that they will be ready for "real" school. In an effort to do everything right, parents turn to the experts and attempt to follow them even though the experts may disagree on what should be done. As a result, the parents are confused.

More and more parents are following advice on what they believe will help the intellectual development of the child, while the other aspects of the child's development are being relegated to a less important role. I believe this is done because intellectual development can be charted, evaluated, observed and taught. Also, parents have many commercial tools at their disposal to help them as they interact with the children in this realm. They can buy books for the children and read to them. They can buy crayons and coloring books and teach them the colors. They can buy scissors and paper to help them with cutting. The list of things to buy is almost endless - games, puzzles, computers. As a result, some children come to school with these skills while others may have been neglected. The problem becomes compounded by the fact that many schools now conduct the kindergarten program as a downward extension of the regular school program so that other important developmental areas are ignored.

Besides intellectual development, we must be concerned with the physical, emotional and social development of the child. These areas seem vague and not as concrete as the intellectual area. They are difficult to evaluate quantitatively, but they are just as important. In addition, there is the danger that if we concentrate on the academic skill aspect of the child's development to the exclusion of the rest, we may be asking children to do tasks that are inappropriate for their level of total development.

Children who by five years old should have had a great deal of experience being physically active. They should have had opportunities to hop, to jump and later, to skip. They should have been helped to develop independence and be now able to wash, to dress and to feed themselves and to use the toilet. They should have had opportunities to play with their peers in dramatic play where they can take on a variety of roles. They should have the beginnings of social skills.

Children need many opportunities to interact with the objects, materials and people in their environment. These activities include block building, measuring, weighing, planting, pouring, filling, playing in the sand box and so on. They are concrete thinkers and need to interact with concrete objects, not just books and pencil and paper. Children should be encouraged to be active and not passive learners.

Children benefit when given opportunities for spontaneous play. This helps them to learn about themselves and others, to learn how to get along with others, and to learn about reality. Children at this age need to be given many opportunities to explore their world. They are not empty vessels to be filled by teachers with facts. They need actual, real-life experiences first before they can deal with abstract concepts. When a child predicts that something will happen, the adult's response should be: "Let's find out." The process of finding out is more important at this level than the correct answer.

Young children need a rich physical environment and space in which to explore this environment. They also need time to integrate and practice new skills. This is best accomplished in an atmosphere that is child-centered and not adult task-oriented. There should be movement, activity, singing, dancing, nurturing, exploring and finding out. Parents can best help their children by providing such an atmosphere at home and by monitoring the programs provided for their children in school settings.

8

Independence

There is a saying in the world of real estate that to successfully buy a house you should consider three things: location, location, location. In the world of parenting to successfully raise children you must do three things: anticipate, anticipate, anticipate. Parents who have learned to do this make their lives easier. Here are just a few examples.

The first thing to anticipate is that your baby is going to become mobile one day. Anticipate that day by childproofing your home. Get down on your hands and knees and see the world from your child's viewpoint. Cover all electrical outlets. Put locks on all closets that have cleaning material in them. Put away or out-of-reach all of your breakable possessions. Notice which pieces of furniture have sharp edges and either cover them or remove them. Anticipation in this instance allows your child to explore his world safely and happily. It is much better than thwarting your child's development by constantly saying "No" to protect him.

The next thing to anticipate is that as your baby grows, he is going to start to develop his own personality and to strive to become independent. In order to do this, he is going to start to say "No" no matter what the request is. You have not failed as a parent. The child needs to do this to grow. The best thing to do is not to make too many verbal requests. When you really want him to do something, pick him up and put him where you want him to be. This works better than a lot of talking and explaining. Too much discussion usually falls on deaf ears. Some parents get upset because they are afraid their child lacks discipline and is thwarting their authority. They then resort to physical punishment. If you anticipate this stage, you will not be threatened and will discipline appropriately.

In the same vein, it helps to anticipate which activities are going to cause difficulty for your child. If he has a short attention span, do not insist that he go shopping with you for two to three hours when you know from past experience that he gets upset and negative. Spanking a child because he gets cranky is not useful especially when you could have predicted the behavior. Anticipating that he will get cranky allows you to take appropriate steps ahead of time.

This applies to other situations where children might have difficulty. Two such situations are visiting relatives, and eating in restaurants. Some relatives have a difficult time with children. They do not take precautions by putting away their favorite vase and get very upset when something gets broken. Anticipate this by asking them to be aware that children like to explore. Or, you could limit the amount of time you stay with those relatives. Most children can control their behavior for just so long. Asking them not to touch anything for four or five hours may be asking too much.

This is also true for taking children out to restaurants. Try it and see how they behave. If they cannot handle it, it is best to take them home immediately and to try again at a later time. Embarrassing you and them in the restaurant is not productive and shows lack of anticipation. You could practice proper behavior at home before trying again.

In order to anticipate behavior, it helps to know about children's developmental stages. Your librarian can recommend many suitable books. It also helps to know your unique child well. When you get good at anticipation, you will find yourself using the "No" word less and less with your children. As a result, their lives and yours will be much more pleasant.

9

Too Soon

In an effort to give the best to our children we sometimes do too much too soon. We are then surprised when things do not turn out as well as we expected. Instead of rushing and planning ahead for our children, we might be more helpful if we took time to find out who they are and gave them time to develop their own unique personalities.

There are a growing number of educational programs for young children that introduce preschoolers to symbolic rules and rote learning too soon. Instead of workbook drills and spelling exercises, the children should be exposed to learning experiences that are self-directed and take into account the children's natural curiosity and motivation. Children who have spent many years in day care programs are not more ready for academic instruction at an earlier age than children who have not had this experience.

Research indicates that readiness and maturity are more critical for success in kindergarten than previous preschool or day care experience. Research also indicates that children who are taught to read at a very early age are no further ahead of their classmates by grade three than those children who were taught later when they were developmentally ready to acquire the skills and knowledge offered.

Adults tend to want to get on with it and speed up the process of learning. Some parents are under the mistaken impression that a child's intelligence is based on how well he can read and use language. Therefore, the reasoning goes, the sooner he learns to read, the more intelligent he will be. This is a very shortsighted definition of intelligence and learning. A child needs to develop many other types of intelligence: linguistic, musical, logical-mathematical, spatial, bodily-kinesthetic and personal. Many children fail to develop in these other areas because adults tend to value only the verbal-academic.

Well-meaning parents need to resist the tendency to give in to advertising which tells them: How to Raise a Brighter Child, Kindergarten is Too Late, How to Teach Your Baby to Read, How to Give Your Baby Encyclopedic Knowledge. More is not better. What is better is to match our teaching to what the children are developmentally ready to learn. Otherwise, we may produce children with poor self-concepts and low motivation to learn. We cannot teach a six-month-old baby to walk if he is not developmentally ready to do so, nor can we teach him to run before he walks.

Parents can best help their children by acknowledging that all children develop and mature at different rates and the rate of development has nothing to do with intelligence. Parents who attempt to accelerate this rate are doing their children a disservice and causing them to be stressed unnecessarily.

Parents may need to monitor the programs their children are being offered at school to be certain that they take into account the developmental level of the children. This is especially true of kindergarten programs.

Schools could solve this problem by eliminating grade designations and calling schools the primary, the intermediate and the high school units. Some children might take five years to complete the primary unit while others might take six or seven. Children who develop on a slower or faster timetable should not be penalized. The goal of schooling should be to help all children reach their fullest potential.

The verb, "to educate", means "to lead", "to draw out", "to develop". It does not imply changing children into something they are not.

10

Decide to Work

Women who leave work to have a child often have a difficult decision to make after the birth of the child. They must decide when to go back to work. It is important that parents have the information necessary for an informed decision. The final decision is theirs and once made, parents should not be made to feel guilty no matter what their decision. Many new parents, however, are uninformed about child development and sometimes make this irrevocable decision based on lack of information.

Dr. Burton White of the Center for Parent Education has worked for over twenty years observing babies from birth to three years of age. His studies indicate that these years are critical for children's ultimate educational development and that the best teachers are the parents and grandparents. These are the people who give the children the incentive to grow and to develop by their deep love and encouragement. They are the baby's first cheering section as each milestone is passed. For the new parents and grandparents, seeing the child learn to take his first step or say his first word produces genuine and delightful fuss in which the baby basks and grows.

Babies need to explore their environment to learn. Their curiosity can decline if they are too restricted. They need someone to watch them so that they can explore safely. They need someone to help them when they get stuck. This takes a commitment on the part of the adult and the people who are most committed are the parents and grandparents.

Dr. White is so convinced of the importance of parents and grandparents in providing care for the first three years of life that he recommends that the government provide support and assistance to the family so that the parents can provide this care rather than providing support for day care centers. He recommends a parent education program for families so that they can provide their children's first educational delivery system. Intervention should begin at the earliest age possible and should improve the child's home environment by sensitizing the parents to the child's developmental needs.

Parents need to know about developmental stages in order to be prepared to help their child develop language and social skills. Part of this preparedness requires that they be alert to physical and sensory handicaps. Dr. White is especially concerned about hearing loss. When it occurs, detecting and responding to the loss is crucial. During the first three years of life, children undergo rapid, basic language learning. Delay in acquiring language skills is one of the most common causes of under-achieving in school. Being able to hear is essential to the development of receptive language in a young baby. Parents need to know about the importance of talking to babies. The baby should begin to understand speech even though she cannot talk herself.

The first three years constitute a once-in-a-lifetime opportunity for the child to attain good language skills in addition to a sense of curiosity about the world around her. Many other essential skills are acquired during this period. It is the time when the child develops a sense of trust and learns that she is loved and safe. The child begins the development of good interpersonal skills. This is not a haphazard process or one that can be left to chance. Dr. White feels it is harder to produce a happy and nice child than it is to produce a smart one. Parents have to make a decision about their children and how they want them to develop. It takes work and commitment but putting the commitment into these first three years will make the rest of the job easier and more successful.

11

Hearing and Language

The first thing to be concerned about is whether your child hears correctly. By three months your child should be startled by a loud clap behind him. By six months he should search for the source of a sound by turning his eyes and head. By ten months he should respond to his own name or to a telephone ringing. By fifteen months he should be able to look at familiar objects when asked to and imitate simple sounds and words. No child is too young for a hearing test. Tests should be given more than once and at different times. If you have concerns or doubts go to a specialist.

Your child should be developing receptive and expressive language skills. Receptive skills refer to how well your child understands language. Expressive skills refer to the production of language. All children understand more than they can or do express. A stimulating environment helps them to develop in both areas. In expressive language development,

☐ by three months he should be babbling,

☐ by six months, he should be expressing eagerness and vocalizing pleasure and displeasure,

☐ by eight months, he should be producing different sounds like "ba", "da", "ka".

- ☐ by ten months, he should be able to shout to attract attention and may say "mamma" and "dada",

- ☐ by twelve months, he should be able to repeat familiar words by imitation.

Dr. Patricia Kuhl of the University of Washington says that mothers who talk "motherese" with its high pitch, exaggerated intonation and clear pronunciation, help babies acquire phonetic prototypes which are the building blocks of language. Parents should talk to their babies often in order for them to hear the sounds which help to develop language.

We could all use a sitter like John Travolta in the movie, "Look Who's Talking". The character played by Travolta took care of the baby for a year. He did not take the easy way out and put the baby in the crib and pacify him with a bottle. Instead, he talked to him constantly. He took him to see an airplane and talked to the baby all of the time about what he was seeing. As Travolta drove the car, he talked through all the actions that he was taking: "first you put the key in, then you push down on the pedals, then you turn the steering wheel." This baby was being stimulated to learn all of the time he was with Travolta.

Dr. Jean Piaget, the Swiss scholar whose greatest research was on how the child develops, would endorse Travolta's method. In his studies of very young children Piaget found that the more new things the baby sees and hears, the more new things he will be interested in seeing and hearing. The idea is to keep the baby interested as he develops. This is the period when the child develops a zest for wonder.

12

Testing and Teaching

The teaching of reading and writing in kindergarten until recently was not permitted. Now we have tests to determine if children are ready for the kindergarten curriculum that includes reading and writing.

Many school systems test children before they come to kindergarten. As a result of these tests some children are declared more ready than others. This can have a devastating affect on the parents. For five years the parents have been very happy watching and helping their child develop. Then the child is given a test, usually lasting less than a half hour, and the parents are led to believe that in some way their child is deficient. He or she is not ready for kindergarten. Parents not only can lose confidence in themselves they can lose confidence in their child. Their wonderful child is somehow wanting in the eyes of the world. It does not matter that the child is performing well within the range of normal development, that the tests have big uncertainties, and that rates of development vary considerably. All the parent takes away from the testing is the feeling that there is something wrong.

One of the goals of the school should be to inspire a parent to have confidence in his or her child. This deep-down parental confidence will carry that child a long way. Schools should be finding ways of demonstrating to parents that their children have a chance to succeed in coping with life, rather than giving a negative message which deprives them of confidence in themselves and their children. Nothing is more disheartening than an expectation of hopelessness and failure for one's own child.

Dr. Harriet Egertson, of the National Association of Early Childhood Specialists, makes a plea for recapturing kindergarten for five-year olds. Twenty years earlier, she reminds us, no one worried whether children had long attention spans, whether they could count to 20, say their ABC's or knew their sounds because it was expected that school would teach these things in good time. There was no imposed kindergarten readiness criteria based on eye-hand coordination or auditory and visual memory because the materials and equipment were designed to help these capacities to emerge.

Today the kindergarten curriculum is at least one year accelerated, requiring the teaching of specific skills that the children are expected to learn. Dr. Egertson goes on to bemoan the fact that rich, creative experiences with real materials like blocks, clay, paint and dramatic play props have been replaced by worksheets, workbooks, and other didactic tasks. She believes that children spend too much time practicing, over and over, a narrow spectrum of discrete skills that are seldom tied to anything young children care about, are interested in, or need. Also many of these tasks are just plain boring which deadens the enthusiasm for learning that children bring with them. Worse, they cause many children to feel like failures.

There used to be a separate certification for teaching kindergarten. Now teachers have one certification for kindergarten to eighth grade. An eighth grade teacher can be reassigned to teach kindergarten with no extra special training.

13

Empathy

Being able to put oneself in another's place, to feel what he feels and to understand what he understands is an attribute necessary for the survival of the human race. Its development is so important that it cannot be left to chance. It has to be consciously modeled and taught. Empathetic adults produce empathetic children.

Parents can help their child to develop this trait by first providing opportunities for him to understand and to practice using words that express feelings. Words like angry, happy, sad can be displayed on the refrigerator door with the appropriate pictures beside them. The child can help pick out pictures that express emotion from magazines or he can draw them himself.

Once the concrete-thinking child understands what the words mean, parents can begin to use them in order to help the child to understand how his actions affect others. "When you hit your brother, he gets upset and cries because it hurts." "Taking your friend's toy without asking makes him feel sad." "I feel happy because you helped me by picking up your toys."

These concepts can be reinforced through stories in books and on television. As you read the story, ask your child how he thinks the character in the story feels and why. If he says the character is sad, ask your child what he would do to make him happy. If one of the characters is mean, ask what he could do to help the mean child not feel so bad. Ask how he would feel if somebody did that to him. Use the breaks provided by commercials to ask the same questions regarding the TV program you are watching. Using TV this way makes it an active and not a passive activity.

If possible, it helps to have a family pet like a cat or dog that the child can relate to and perhaps be responsible for. A pet responds to kindness with affection. A mistreated animal, on the other hand, responds by becoming withdrawn or by being aggressive. These responses give children concrete, almost instantaneous feedback, that all actions, both positive and negative have consequences.

Cruelty to animals, especially in young children, needs to be given attention. They either do not understand that the animal is suffering or they do understand and they do not care. These are the children who may have never been given the opportunity to experience empathy in their own lives.

On the other hand, it tells you a great deal about a person when he is kind to an animal. Movies use this fact to develop a character's personality quickly. If they want the macho man to have a tender side, they show him taking care of his cat.

Schools can help children by providing opportunities for them not only to experience empathy, but to practice it. This can be done through cooperative learning lessons, school counsels, older children reading to younger ones, food and clothing drives, visiting nursing homes, and so on.

Parents can tell their own stories about how somebody helped them that day or how they helped or understood somebody else. Children should be noticed and encouraged every time they give the empathetic response rather than the negative, mean one. They should be encouraged to tell how it makes them feel when they respond positively to another.

It is never too early to begin to develop empathy in children. Professor Alan Leslie of Rutgers University, in studying the development of perception in infants and young children, found that what can be observed developing in infants becomes a recognizable trait by three to four years of age. By even that young age, a child can infer what another child perceives even though that perception is different from his own.

14

Self-esteem

There is no guaranteed, successful method to ensure that your child will develop positive self-esteem since it is not something you give to a child. He either develops it or he does not. You can, however, promote an atmosphere where it can be nurtured. Children are concrete thinkers and are very observant. Adults are their models. If you model positive self-esteem, it can become catching. Parents who are fearful about making mistakes have a difficult time finding joy and relaxing around their children. The more joy, fun and laughter you can bring into the home, the more your chances are of having happy children who feel good about themselves.

Try to slow down especially when dealing with very young children. Relax with your babies. Babies need to be able to explore their environments safely on their own terms. They need to be encouraged in these explorations and not thwarted. This is the time when babies learn about themselves, their world and become creative explorers. Babies who do not have these opportunities become passive. Parents need only to relax and to be available to take the cues from the baby. You do not need to accelerate this development. Give him time and rejoice in every milestone and he will get there on his own time frame.

Try not to compare his rate of development to others in the family or to the baby down the street. Each child is unique. As the saying goes: Childhood is a Journey not a Race. This is the time in your child's development when you can really relax and enjoy yourself because babies know what they need to do in order to prosper. It only becomes a problem when the parents' agenda interferes with the baby's agenda. We sometimes are in too much of a hurry to get on with it. Not only with the babies' development but with getting and keeping the house perfect or trying to raise perfect children like the children down the street.

We become involved in doing things for the children but not enjoying or taking the time to be with them as persons. Have confidence in yourself and relax and instead of painting the kitchen, sit beside the sandbox, give your child your undivided attention and encourage him to explore. If the lady down the street has children but spends most of her time keeping her house perfect, stop visiting her. Find somebody who is also sitting beside the sandbox letting her child know she enjoys giving him, her undivided attention.

Improve your own self-esteem so that you are a good role model. I hate to tell you but you still cannot get away with: Do as I say, not as I do. When you hear about self-esteem, it always seems to be a case of: "If only the rest of the world would do better by me, I would be okay." It always seems to be dependent on someone else's behavior not your own. You cannot control what the rest of the world will do or not do so you must take responsibility for how you feel about yourself. Once you learn to do this, you can help your children. One way to do this is to distinguish between rational and irrational beliefs.

Irrational:

- ☐ Everybody must love me.

- ☐ I must be good at everything.

- ☐ Some people are bad and must be punished.

- ☐ Things should be different.

- ☐ It's your fault I feel this way.

- [ ] I know something bad will happen soon.

- [ ] It's easier not to even try.

- [ ] I can't help being this way.

- [ ] I need someone stronger than I am.

- [ ] I need to get upset about your problems.

- [ ] There's only one good way to do it.

Rational:

- [ ] Everybody does not have to love me.

- [ ] It is okay to make mistakes.

- [ ] I do not have to control things.

- [ ] I am responsible for my day.

- [ ] I can handle it when things go wrong.

- [ ] It is important to try.

- [ ] I am capable.

- [ ] I can change.

- [ ] Other people are capable.

- [ ] I can be flexible.

The same parents who are very effective in the workplace and feel good about themselves may not feel good about themselves as parents.

You are the expert as far as your own children are concerned. Trust your judgment. Mistakes may be made, but if we learn from them, they are not failures. The problem for parents today is that there are too many uncontrollable negative outside influences that impact the family. Just to name a few: television, insecure job opportunities, job stress, overworked and overtired parents, world catastrophes, no pleasant or upbeat news in the papers or television, guns in the hands of young people who do not hesitate to use them, and youth gangs. You can add to the list

In order to survive in the world today, all members of the family need to help one another to develop and to nurture self-esteem. The family is the place where all members should be accepted completely as they are, not as they might be, could be, should be--but as they are. This acceptance allows them to go back into the world renewed and able to face most challenges.

15

Praise and Encouragement

All members of the family need to practice encouraging behavior. This includes father to mother, mother to father as well as among the children. When people are only told how incompetent they are, they cease to learn and refuse to take risks. All members of the family need to be told and to be encouraged when they do things right, not just caught and told when they do things wrong.

Start with yourself. Compliment yourself instead of finding fault. "I look good today. That color looks nice on me." Do the same with your family at breakfast. "Mary, I like the way you did your hair. You look nice." "Joe, thanks for getting me the paper. I appreciate your noticing I wanted it." Model accepting compliments. If your husband compliments you on how you are dressed, thank him and avoid making negative comments like, "how could you like this old thing?" If somebody says you did something well, say, "Yes I think so, too," rather than, "Oh, it was nothing."

These words of encouragement should be given constantly -- ten to fifteen times a day at least. Words of encouragement give the message that in your family everyone is accepted as they are, not for what they could or should be. Treat each child uniquely, not equally.

There is a difference between praise and encouragement. Praise is a label and all labels should be avoided. Praise attaches conditional love to behavior. "I'm proud of you. You came in first." "You are a good girl." To build self-esteem, focus on behavior that is appreciated rather than imply that children have more worth as persons if they excel. Children must feel that their person is cherished, independent of their behavior. This is called separating the deed from the doer. Examples kinds of labels tend to stick: "Sally is slow developing. Her sister walked much sooner." Other examples of negative are labels are: uncommunicative, shy, slow, unfeeling, and unaffectionate. Describe behavior but do not label. "Sally has a difficult time in new situations. It takes her awhile to warm up, but she does eventually when she feels comfortable. I usually give her more time to get used to new things instead of forcing her to do it right away." Sally may grow out of the behavior, but all of her life she could be stuck with the label of the shy one in the family and find it difficult to change this impression and perhaps develop into a different person.

Learn to use "I" statements and not "You" statements. Never say anything against the child as a person. You can say negative things about the behavior but you accept the child completely as he is, not as he might be, could be, should be--but as he is. He or she is the best thing that ever happened to your family. The "you" statement places blame and labels the child. It is a verbal attack against the person. The "I" statement on the other hand tells how you feel and how the behavior affects you. Describe what you see, what you feel, what you expect. Do not humiliate your child, attack his character or offend his dignity.

"You" statement: "You idiot, look what you did by not watching where you are going. You broke the lamp." "I" statement: "I am upset because the lamp is broken. The next time, put on the light before you look for something in the room." In families, labels tend to stick. If you label the child as a bad person that is what you will get. Remember to treat each child uniquely, not equally. Children are born with different temperaments the same way parents come with different temperaments. Accept and rejoice in these differences and understand them so that your children can develop into the people they were meant to be not into the people you want them to be. Children can develop poor self-esteem when they get the message that their parents wanted a different child from the one they got. A child may get the distinct message that his parents would rather have a gifted soccer player like the kid next door, or a popular cheer leader like the girl down the street, instead of the introverted loner they have who is not like either of his out-going parents. These different temperaments affect how parents respond to each child, how they discipline and how they respond to different child rearing practices.

Provide opportunities for your children to make choices. They need to feel some control over their lives. Along with choice comes accepting the consequences of these choices. Of course, you cannot allow them to come to harm, but otherwise, try not to step in to protect children when their choices do not turn out well. This shows a lack of confidence in them and does not help build self-esteem.

16

Finally

Teach your children to become problem solvers. Competent problem solvers feel good about themselves and children can learn to solve most problems themselves. Resist the temptation to step in and to make the world perfect. The world is not perfect. You know this and have learned that it is okay. You can handle it. Help your children do the same.

Ask yourself the question: Are we as a family enjoying each other and having fun? If the answer is no, rethink what you are doing. Think of ways to bring fun and joy to your life and to your family's life. There has to be someplace where people can be renewed and accepted completely. The best possibility is in the family. Life is too sad otherwise and it does not have to be that way. This might be the time to examine your priorities. I wish you joy as you experience life's greatest adventure -- nurturing and raising children who feel and experience your love.

Index

Harriet Egertson, An independent consultant, a former kindergarten and primary teacher.
Early Childhood Specialists.

Patricia Kuhl, University of Washington:
Speech & Hearing Sciences

Alan Leslie, Rutgers University:
Development of perception in infants and young children.

Jean Piaget, University of Geneva:
Theory of Cognitive Development

John Travolta, Actor, "Look Who's Talking":
"…took care of the baby for a year…"

Burton White, Harvard Graduate School of Education, Tufts Universities, Brandeis Universities:
Early Childhood Education

James Q. Wilson, UCLA:
Political Scientist, Public Administration, Sociology.

Other Books by Dr. Devlin

Arrows Swift and Far
"Guiding Your Child through School"

and

Cassandra's Classroom
"Innovative Solutions for Education Reform"

For other articles by Dr. Devlin
visit her blog:
www.cassandrasclassroom.org

About the Author

Dr. Nancy Devlin is a psychologist, educator, author and lecturer. For twelve years, her column, "Today's Parents," addressed education and family issues and appeared weekly in New Jersey's Star Ledger. She has also written for the Princeton Packet Newspapers.

Dr. Devlin is a licensed psychologist, a family therapist and a nationally-certified school psychologist. Her professional history includes teaching elementary school in New York City, Long Island and in military-dependent schools in Germany, Denmark, and Japan. She was a staff member at the Educational Testing Service and lecturer at Rutgers University. She was a psychologist for 22 years in the Princeton school system. At present she is a writer, counseling parents, and students and lobbying for better educational systems.

She graduated from Hunter College with a degree in English and went on to obtain a Masters degree from Hunter College in Guidance and School Counseling. She earned a Ph.D. in Educational Psychology at the University of California at Berkeley.

Born in Jenkintown, Pennsylvania, Dr. Devlin lives in Philadelphia. She is married to a physicist, and they have three sons.

Printed in the United States
By Bookmasters